C000057777

Illustrations credits:
Archivio White Star/Marcello Bertinetti:
Cover, back cover, pages 2-3, 7, 8-9, 10-11, 13, 20-21, 24, 26 right, 30-31, 35, 38-39, 40-41, 44, 46 right, 51, 52-53, 55 right, 58, 63, 66, 68, 73, 74-75, 77, 80, 82, 83, 88, 90, 94, 95, 96.
Archivio White Star/Carlo De Fabianis:
Pages 1, 12, 16, 19, 25, 26 left, 32-33, 36-37, 45, 49, 54, 64, 72, 81, 84, 91, 92.
Archivio White Star/Angela White Bertinetti:
Pages 4, 6, 15, 17, 18, 22-23, 34, 42-43, 46 left, 47, 48, 50, 55 left, 62, 67, 76, 78, 79, 85, 87 bottom.
Jean-Charles Pinheira:
Pages 14, 17, 18, 28-29, 56-57, 59, 60, 61, 65, 69, 70-71, 86, 87 top, 89, 93.

ⓒ 1991 White Star
Via C. Sassone 24, Vercelli, Italy.

All rights reserved. Reproduction of the whole or any part of the contents, without written permission, is prohibited.

Printed and bound in Singapore.

First published in English in 1991 by Tiger Books International PLC, London.
ISBN 1-85501-174-3

Translated by
Patricia Borlenghi

Edited by
Heather Thomas

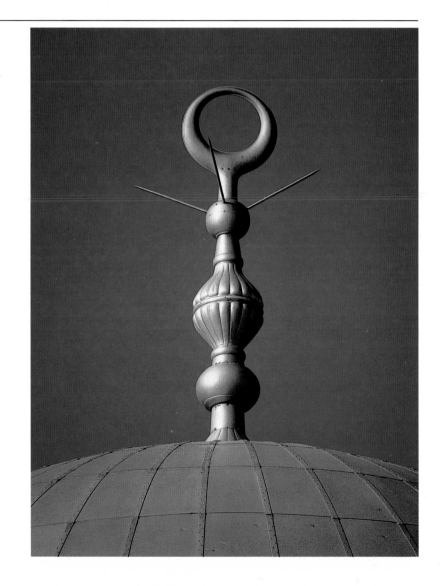

INSIDE
JERUSALEM

TEXT
PATRIZIA RAFFIN

DESIGN
PATRIZIA BALOCCO

TIGER BOOKS INTERNATIONAL

2-3 At sunset in Jerusalem, the fading sun illuminates the Old and New quarters of the city. Nestling in the Judean Hills on the edge of the desert, it is one of the world's most ancient and holy cities.

4 The summit of the Dome of the Rock, one of the holiest shrines in the world for Moslems and Jews. The oldest monument in the Islamic world, it was built in AD 691 on the site of the great Temple of Solomon where Abraham was prepared to sacrifice his son Isaac, and Mohammed took off on his ride up to heaven.

6 To the south-west of the Old City is Mount Zion, a place of pilgrimage for Jews and Christians alike.

7 This aerial view of Jerusalem shows the proximity of the desert and mountains to the city.

8-9 The characteristically golden local Judaic stone blends so well with the surrounding desert that it seems to disappear almost chameleon-like into its natural surroundings.

Jerusalem is among the world's most ancient cities. In Abraham's time it was known by the Egyptians as *Urushamen* or, in Hebrew, *Yerushalayim*. Some scholars believe that this name was derived from *Yerah* meaning a city, and *Shalom* meaning peace, and thus it is still known as the city of peace. However, it is more likely that it means the city founded by the god Salem or the local lord Shalem who ruled the city around 2500 BC. Many historians still favour the first explanation, but ironically never was a city more disputed, besieged, threatened and thrown into turmoil than Jerusalem.

The city's ancient past is well known, albeit mixed with legend, and is recorded for posterity in the Bible. However, its more recent history, from the late nineteenth century, is interwoven with the lives of two people - Theodor Herzl, the founder of modern Zionism, and Chaim Weizman, who played a leading role in the negotiations that led to the Balfour Declaration of 1917 and later became the first President of Israel. With the British Protectorate of Palestine drawing to a close in 1947, there were fierce struggles between Zionists and Arab nationalists. The United Nations ratified the partitioning of the territory into two states, one Jewish and the other Arab, declaring Jerusalem to be a free city with international status. However, the fierce fighting continued and, with the British evacuation in 1948, the new state of Israel was proclaimed, with Jerusalem as its capital. But while the Western part of the city was Israeli territory, the Old City in the Eastern quarter remained in Jordanian hands.

The rest is recent history. During the Six Day War in June 1967, the Israelis took possession of the entire city and officially annexed it on 28 June of that year. The barbed wire and barricades of the divided city were torn down and under the direction of its charismatic mayor, Teddy Kollek, the city embarked on an ambitious building and development project financed by international Jewry through the Jerusalem Foundation. Parks, museums, galleries, housing, shopping centres and stadia sprung up in the city. But even today, you can sense the divisions and the underlying tension that exist between Moslem East Jerusalem and Jewish West Jerusalem. Christians and Arabs account for one-third of the city's 475,000 inhabitants; the remainder being made up of secular and Orthodox Jews. With the Arab uprising (the *Intifada*) in the Occupied Territories spilling over into Jerusalem itself, it is still a city in search of what may be an unattainable peace. In Jerusalem you enter the realms of the past and literally live and breathe its unique history. The young native Israelis born in Israel since 1948 are called *Sabras*, a name derived from the prickly pear with its tough exterior but tender interior. They are the new pioneers, believing in and working for a young, proud nation, whether on the ancient streets of Jerusalem, in the *kibbutzim* or in the smart commercial district of Tel Aviv. What Jerusalem offers to the Sabra is the continuity between past and present, and the inner strength that will be necessary to complete the task entrusted to him. For the Sabra, the past is most poignantly symbolized by the Wailing Wall where people come to pray and mourn the past and its dead and at Yad Vashem, the memorial to the Holocaust and its six million Jewish victims who were exterminated by the Nazis during World War II. Here the young Sabra can pray for the birth of a new and better world.

10-11 In urban Jerusalem, the Old City districts make a stark contrast to the modern office blocks and hotels springing up around them. Since the reunification of East and West Jerusalem in 1967, there has been a steady rise in commercial and residential development projects. The suburbs now reach out as far as the Judean desert itself.

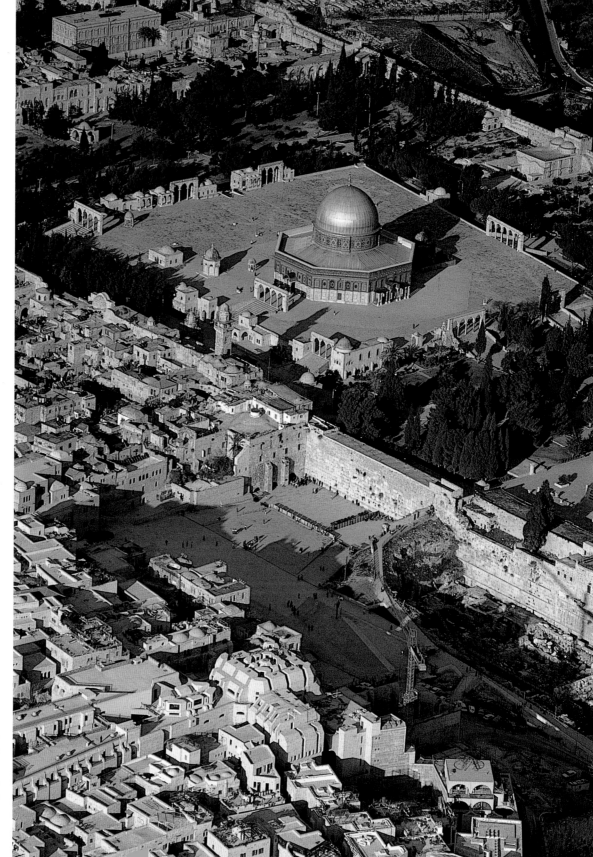

12 The new high-rise buildings are starting to encroach on the Old City with its narrow streets and ancient religious sites and monuments.

13 The gold cupola and brilliant blue mosaics of the Dome of the Rock crown Harem esh-Sharif, or the Temple Mount, in the east of the Old City.

14 The Damascus Gate, here shown crowded with people, is the major point of access from northern Jerusalem to the Old Town. Built by Suleiman the Magnificent between 1537 and 1540, it is one of only three gates, together with the Jaffa and Lion gates, that still retain their original structure. It was erected for defensive purposes and its huge towers and corridor-like entrance were designed to repulse and slow down any potential attackers.

15 Wine is still produced in Jerusalem. Many Israeli wines are too sweet for the drier palates of Europeans and Americans but you can buy some fine full-bodied reds and good semi-dry whites.

16-17 The Moslem Quarter in the north and east of the Old City has changed very little over the centuries. Here the men still dress in traditional robes and keffikahs (Arab head-dress).

18 With its maze of narrow streets and alleys, the Moslem Quarter is the largest and most densely populated part of the Old City. It is a colourful district with souks, money-changers, carpet-sellers, pastry shops and felafel stalls. The years seem to have passed this quarter by and life continues in the time-honoured way.

18

19 Jerusalem is a city of great contrasts – especially between the old and the new. Young Israelis in modern Western-style dress pass women in traditional costume from a by-gone age on the same street.

20 You can buy almost anything in the Moslem Quarter's souk. Here you will find not only fresh fruit and vegetables but also Bedouin carpets, ornate jewellery, old coins, Arab robes and glassware. Never pay the quoted price – you are expected to haggle with the shopkeepers to get yourself a bargain.

21 From the bakeries wafts an inviting aroma of delicious freshly baked pita and other speciality breads.

22-23 To the north-east of the Old Town and the Damascus Gate is Mount Scopus, home of the New Hebrew University. From this high point you can enjoy a spectacular view of not only the Old City but also the desert, the mountains and even the distant Dead Sea.

24 *The Arabs call the magnificent fortified Damascus Gate Bab-el-Amud, meaning 'the gate of the pillars', as it was from one of these pillars that the distance between Jerusalem and Damascus was measured. The name may also be derived from the time when the city was known by its Roman name – Aelia Capitolina – and a column or pillar signified the entrance to a city.*

25 *The Jaffa Gate was also erected by Suleiman the Magnificent and earned its name from its position at the beginning of the trade route between Jerusalem and the important Mediterranean port of Jaffa.*

Prayers are said at the Wailing Wall, especially on the Sabbath, national holidays and days of mourning. On Monday and Thursday mornings the Torah is read aloud, and it is on these days that many boys gather here to be bar mitzvahed. For all Jews everywhere the Wailing Wall holds a special religious and symbolic importance as it was one of the retaining walls of the Second Temple of Herod the Great built on the site of the original great Temple of Solomon.

27 The scrolls of the Torah are carried ceremoniously in procession through the crowds of believers to the Wailing Wall. Several prayer services may be held simultaneously here by different groups of Jews.

28-29 During the prayers, the scrolls of the Torah are solemnly unrolled and then read aloud to the assembled worshippers.

32-33 The Garden of Gethsemane where Jesus prayed the night before his arrest lies at the foot of the Mount of Olives to the east of the Old Town. The Church of the Nations, designed by Antonio Barluzzi in 1924 and paid for by the donations of twelve countries, is one of the most notable buildings. In the background you can see the distinctive onion-shaped domes of the Russian church of Mary Magdalene, founded by the Tsar Alexander III as a memorial to his mother, the Tsarina Maria Alexandrovna.

34 Mount Zion is crowned by the Church of the Dormition, built by German Benedictines in 1910. Its distinctive black cone-shaped roof is a local landmark, but inside, the Byzantine influence is strongest, displayed especially in the splendour of the magnificent mosaics.

35 The Mosque of Al-Aksa with its unmistakable silver dome rises above the Old City on the Temple Mount. The interior is truly majestic although little remains of the original mosque. The twelve white Carrara marble columns were donated by Mussolini while the ceiling they support was presented by the Egyptian king Farouk. The cupola itself is richly decorated with mosaics and the floors are covered with priceless oriental carpets.

*I*f, in the collective imagination, Rome is the cradle of Western civilization and New York the vibrant symbol of the modern age, then Jerusalem represents the Holy City - the pilgrim's way that exists within us all. Certainly most of the attractions and entertainment forms that can be found in other cities are not present in Jerusalem. The city literally lives in its religious past which bestows upon it a unique identity and diversity. Even the most sceptical disbeliever visiting Jerusalem for the first time soon becomes aware of this special quality that sets it apart from other cities in the East and West.

The great shrines and holy places of Judaism, Islam and Christianity cannot help but move the most ardent disbeliever. This emotional 'conversion' may be brought about when treading the well-worn sightseeing path between the Wailing Wall, the Mount of Olives, the Coenaculum (the scene of the Last Supper), the Church of the Holy Sepulchre, the Dome of the Rock and on the Via Dolorosa following the Stations of the Cross. The memories of the dust-laden past may even be sufficiently evocative to inspire a new spiritual reawakening in the visitors of the 1990s.

Every day, people of all races, nationalities and faiths walk the streets of Jerusalem. They tread the same path as Christ did nearly 2000 years ago as he carried his cross from his interrogation by Pontius Pilate to Calvary; they watch men praying and meditating at the Wailing Wall on the holy day of Yom Kippur; and listen to the voices of the *muezzin* calling the faithful to prayer. No visitor to the city of David can remain insensitive to the unique atmosphere of this holiest of cities. If you are visiting Jerusalem for the first time, prepare yourself for an unforgettable experience. It is advisable to

spend only a small part of your stay in the New City so that you can prolong your exploration of the Old City. A good place to start is in Jerusalem's financial and commercial centre in the Western part of the city. The three main roads, Jaffa Road, King George Street and Ben-Yehuda Street, form a triangle here in the heart of the New City around Zion Square where ardent Zionists used to meet before independence. Leading off the square around Salamon Street are narrow alleys of shops and restaurants, but if you take the Ben-Yehuda exit you will enter a modern open-air shopping mall, or *midrahov*. Here you can sit and relax at one of the tables in the popular pavement cafes and watch the world go by over a coffee and a snack.

Walking along King George Street you will find the Yeshurun Central Synagogue, the largest in the city, with its important library which is open to the public between 4 and 9pm from Sundays to Thursdays. Further down the street is the Hakhal Shlomo, the seat of the Chief Rabbinate - a religious court. Also housed in this building is the Wolfson Museum with its collection of ritual Jewish artefacts and ceremonial art. Turn into Mamillah Street and stroll down to Independence Park with its green lawns, herbaceous borders and pine trees. Here, in one of Jerusalem's largest parks, people picnic on the grass and go for a stroll on Shabbat. Near the park is the Moslem cemetery with the tombs of some of Saladin's soldiers, and an ancient water cistern – the Mamillah Pool.

Every corner of Jerusalem is steeped in history and resounds to distant echoes of past events. Go down King David Street and you will pass the Bloomfield Garden, the site of Herod's family grave. Turn into the Valley of Hinnom, or Sinners Valley as it is

36 Top left: The Jaffa Gate is guarded by two defensive towers which form part of the Citadel.

36 Bottom left: The Damascus Gate, the most important in Jerusalem, is characterized by the constant flow of people passing through it, which ceases only at nightfall.

36 Right: The Lion Gate, the last of the trio built by Suleiman the Magnificent, was constructed following a dream of the sultan in which he was commanded to build a wall around the city or be devoured by lions.

37 The high golden walls near the Jaffa Gate once protected the Holy City from attackers.

38-39 After Mecca and Medina, the Dome of the Rock is the third most holy Islamic place. Founded by the Omayyad Caliph Abd el-Malikin in AD 691, it is a perfectly symmetrical octagonal building. Although the original cupola was covered in pure gold, it is now constructed of gilded bronze-aluminium and has come to symbolize the city of Jerusalem around the world.

sometimes called, which forms the divide between the old and new cities. This was once the site of a heathen temple where child sacrifices were made. The Hebrew name for the valley, *Ge'Hinnom*, became synonymous with Hell. Indeed the Moslem word for Hell is *Gahannam*. However, now the Hinnom Valley is a centre for the arts and entertainment, with the Khan Theatre, a nightclub, the Jerusalem Cinematheque, some restaurants and crafts galleries.

Follow the road as it bends around and you will come to Mount Zion which has symbolic significance for both Christians and Jews. Here is the Coenaculum where Jesus and his disciples celebrated the Passover meal at the Last Supper. The mountain is crowned by the exquisite Benedictine Church of the Dormition built in 1910 on the site where Mary is reputed to have fallen into eternal sleep. From the high bell tower of this beautiful Romanesque-style church, you can enjoy a splendid view of Jerusalem and the surrounding mountains and desert. South-east of the church lies King David's Tomb, a traditional place of pilgrimage for Jews from all over the world. Upstairs in the same building is the Coenaculum with its vaulted ceiling and stone arches. It is, in fact, part of a fourteenth-century church built by the Crusaders on the site of the building where the Last Supper of Christ and the disciples was held. The room is relatively small and some visitors are disappointed by its sparse and ordinary appearance. It was here also that the resurrected Christ came to sit among his disciples at Pentecost and where they began to speak in tongues. At the back of the Tomb of David below is the Chamber of the Holocaust – a memorial to the millions of Jews killed by the Nazis. Inside the dark

chamber, lit only by candles, are some of the original cremation furnaces, desecrated Torah scrolls and other horrific exhibits from the death camps. Women are refused admission and men must cover their heads before entering. If you retrace your steps back up King David's Street, you can climb the 150-foot high YMCA Tower for a panoramic view of Mount Zion and the city. From this high vantage point, you can see the Citadel with the Tower of David, the Church of the Holy Sepulchre and the golden cupola of the Dome of the Rock. And on the horizon, you can make out the Mount of Olives with the Chapel of Ascension and, to the left, Mount Scopus and the Hebrew University. It is a magnificent view and well worth the climb.

40 Inside the Dome of the Rock, the Holy Rock itself rises out of the ground in stark contrast to the magnificent dome lavishly decorated with 45,000 golden mosaic tiles, some of which are inscribed with verses from the Koran. The original sixteenth-century tiles were replaced in 1963 with the ones that you can see here.

41 The outside of the dome, plated in bronze-aluminium, is over 108 feet high. On the walls beneath the dome, the predominantly blue ceramic tiles complete the facade, which was restored under the auspices of King Hussein of Jordan and completed in 1963.

42-43 A Jewish wedding is a joyous occasion for all the family and is still celebrated in the traditional manner. Relatives and friends often pin money onto the bride's dress and there is much singing and dancing. The family is universally revered and, together with the state of Israel, is the institution most dear to Jews. Marriage is subject to religious jurisdiction – there is no civil marriage ceremony or divorce available in Jerusalem.

*T*he Mea She'arim quarter to the north of Zion Square in Western Jerusalem deserves a special mention. Founded by a group of Jewish settlers in 1873 outside the walls of the Old City, it is home to the city's ultra-Orthodox Jewish community. Most are of central and eastern European origin and they still dress in the traditional manner: the bearded men in long black coats and fur or broad-brimmed hats; the women modestly cover up in long dresses with long sleeves and high necks. Many wear a scarf or wig to cover their hair or even shave their heads. Here time seems to have stood still as in a daguerreotype of a late-nineteenth century ghetto. The *haredim*, meaning God-fearing, who live in modern apartments in the maze of narrow streets, seek to protect their spirituality in the modern materialistic world. Their sobre dress and manner reflect their desire to live modestly and devoutly in accordance with the teachings of the Torah. Visitors to Mea She'arim are also expected to respect and observe the customs of the quarter, especially women who are exhorted by posters in English and Hebrew to wear suitably modest dress that will not offend the local residents.

Numerous synagogues and *yeshivot* (Talmudic religious schools) exist here – more than in any other part of the city. The residents strictly observe the rules of the Holy Scriptures, especially those that forbid the violation of the sacredness of the Sabbath. Roadblocks are even erected to prevent traffic entering the quarter, all work stops and peace descends on the usually bustling streets until nightfall on Saturday. The ultra-Orthodox still speak Yiddish and fanatically refuse to recognise the Jewish state of Israel and the Zionist philosophy. They believe that a Jewish state should be

established only when the Biblical prophesies have been fulfilled with the coming of the Messiah. Until such a time, they refuse to accept the validity of the Israeli state, decline to serve in the military forces, and recognise only religious laws. Mea She'arim is like a state within a state – an enclave strongly rooted in its own traditions and zealously guarding its past. A visit to this unique and fascinating district will leave you with unforgettable memories. Leaving the Orthodox Jewish quarter behind, you can continue walking to the Biblical Zoo on Yermiyahu Street with its collection of all the animals mentioned in the Bible. A popular attraction for children, it is open every day between 9am and sunset. While you are in West Jerusalem you should try to visit the covered Machaneh Yehuda Market with its wide range of fruit, vegetable, fish, meat and felafel stores. It is especially busy on Thursdays and Fridays when the Orthodox Jews shop enthusiastically for the Sabbath to enrich their usually frugal tables in honour of the holy day. Stalls stay open from dawn to dusk and the market is always busy and crowded with shoppers. Heading south-west, you will soon reach the Knesset, the Israeli parliament, standing on a small hill in the governmental Hakirya district. In front of the entrance is the Menorah, a seven-branched bronze candelabra which has become the symbol of the modern state of Israel. Important events from Jewish history are displayed upon it. Many world-famous artists have helped to decorate the interior of the Knesset. Marc Chagall designed the great tapestry in the foyer showing the Creation, the Exodus and the Return, and also the wall and floor mosaics. The white stone wall behind the podium in the plenary chamber was designed by Danny Caravan.

44

44 At the Small Wall, a section of the Temple Mount's Western Wall near the Iron Gate, many Jews gather to pray in a more peaceful atmosphere than that of the Wailing Wall where the zealous rabbis, Orthodox Jews, soldiers and civilians all offer up their prayers. It is every practising Jew's most dear wish to pray here beside the huge stone blocks of the 50-foot high wall. It is particularly crowded here on Tisha ba'Av, the anniversary of the destruction of the great Temple.

Many internationally acclaimed artists, sculptors and architects have participated in the creation of the new Jerusalem. In doing so they have masterfully complemented the ancient architecture with modern buildings of light and gold-coloured stone. The striking white dome of the Shrine of the Book which houses the Dead Sea Scrolls, is a particularly fine example of this. The Israel Museum in the city's Givat Ram district is not only home to the famous scrolls but it also exhibits collections of Jewish ceremonial art, ancient pottery, weapons and other artefacts from the many archaeological digs in the region, and paintings by the great European masters from Rembrandt to Picasso and Miró. There is even a Sculpture Garden with celebrated works by Rodin and Henry Moore. Also at Givat Ram is the New Hebrew University standing on the slopes of Mount Scopus.

The final place of pilgrimage for visitors to West Jerusalem is Yad Vashem, the memorial to the Holocaust. You approach it through an avenue of 6000 trees, each representing a Gentile who risked his life to save Jews from the Nazi death camps. The museum records the history of the Holocaust, while nearby is the Hall of Names with its poignant roll-call of those who died, and also the candlelit Hall of Remembrance where the names of the camps are recorded for posterity on the stone floor. Most haunting of all is the Children's Memorial recalling the 1,500,000 children who perished. To visit Yad Vashem is an unforgettable experience but it may help you to understand the character of the modern Israeli – the Sabra with the tough exterior and the warm heart. The memory of the Holocaust is etched deeply into his whole being.

45 Two faces of Jerusalem: the Wailing Wall in the
foreground which is venerated by the Jews, and,
behind it, the Dome of the Rock, one of the holiest
places of Islam.

46-47 Israeli women soldiers are a common sight in Jerusalem, as in other parts of Israel. In the Israeli military no distinction is made between the sexes, and both men and women undergo compulsory military service at eighteen years of age. Only Arabs and the ultra-Orthodox, together with some religious girls, are exempt. The training is tough and exacting but most young women are proud to serve their new country in this way and look forward to their military service. Even when they have completed their service, Israelis still continue to participate as reservists – usually for one month each year.

48-49 Large areas of the old Jewish Quarter were destroyed during the War of Independence in 1948-49. They remained under Jordanian jurisdiction until the Six Day War in 1967 when the Israelis seized the Old City of Jerusalem. The original buildings date from the second half of the eighteenth century and were constructed by Jewish settlers from central and eastern Europe. Orthodox and secular Jews live here side by side in an uneasy coexistence. Even here there are new housing and urban developments, but the architects have tried to adapt traditional styles and building materials so that they blend into their older surroundings. Here, in the quiet squares and plazas, the children play and many Jewish families enjoy the sunshine.

50 Even some young Jewish men wear the traditional long beard favoured by some Orthodox Hassidic religious sects.

51 The Machaneh Yehuda Market on Jaffa Road is patronized mainly by Orthodox Jews. On the eve of the Sabbath the crowds grow noticeably larger as people stock up with fresh food for the weekly Sabbath family dinner.

52-53 Ben Yehuda Mall off Zion Square is lined with shops and open-air cafes and is a popular meeting-place for many young Jews. During the religious holiday of the Tu B'Shevat, the New Year Festival of the Trees, in late January or early February, people go out and plant trees, even in the heart of the city where processions and ceremonies are often held.

54 The huge Church of the Holy Sepulchre, in Jerusalem's Christian Quarter, is the holiest site in all Christendom, with the last Five Stations of the Cross within its walls, including Calvary itself. It huddles among the narrow streets and alleys of this old quarter of the city, and is the ultimate stop and the end of the journey for every Christian pilgrim visiting Jerusalem.

55 Every Friday throughout the year, the Franciscans lead a procession along the Via Dolorosa beginning at the First Station of the Cross on the site of the Roman Antonia Fortress. It follows the route that Jesus took on his walk from his trial to the place of the crucifixion and entombment. Pilgrims can still retrace his steps and even carry a replica cross to the final Stations inside the Church of the Holy Sepulchre.

56-57 Ethiopian pilgrims walk in procession through the Old City along the Via Dolorosa. The Ninth Station of the Cross is inside the entrance of the Ethiopian Coptic Church where Jesus stumbled and fell for the third time. Together with the Armenians, Copts, Orthodox Syrians, Roman Catholics and Greek Orthodox faiths, the Ethiopians make up the Christian communities of Jerusalem.

58-59 The Crusader-built Church of the Holy Sepulchre is divided between several Christian denominations – the Greek Orthodox, Roman Catholics, Armenians, Copts, Ethiopians and Orthodox Syrians, and the many chapels reflect the diversity of these different communities. The interior is lit by candles and ornate lamps donated by popes, kings and emperors, and is very exotic and lavishly decorated in the Eastern style. At the centre of the rotunda is the Holy Sepulchre itself. Pilgrims can pray at one of the many chapels and altars including the Chapel of the Angels where the angel appeared to Mary Magdalene; the Chapel of the Copts; the Chapel of the Sharing of the Raiment; the Chapel of Adam; the Nails of the Holy Cross Altar; and the Crucifixion Altar. Each one has special significance.

*J*erusalem is a city of three religions, and the districts and their communities in the Old City are segregated by religious faith and race. In the north-western part is the Christian Quarter, situated between the Jaffa, New and Damascus Gates. In the south-east, by the Wailing Wall, is the Jewish Quarter. In the north-east and east, including Harem esh-Sharif and the Dome of the Rock, is the Moslem Quarter, while in the south-west behind the Citadel and Tower of David is the Armenian Quarter. Jerusalem has been partitioned in this way for centuries, and it used to be the case that people lived and worked exclusively within their own district. However, although there is not the same pressure to do this today and many people have moved out into the 'New City', the segregation remains and you cannot fail to notice it if you walk around the Altstadt (Old Town). As you cross from one quarter into another you will observe marked cultural differences.

Starting a tour of the Old City at the Jaffa Gate, you must visit the Citadel with its Tower of David. The ancient ruins of the fortified Citadel have been turned into a museum recording the history of Jerusalem through the ages. Heading south-west, you will enter the Armenian Quarter with its ornately decorated St James Cathedral. Enter this immensely beautiful chuirch and you will be transported into a serene and peaceful world of incense, candles, altars and little chapels. On leaving the church, pass the Orthodox Syrian church of St Mark and you will reach David Street with its oriental bazaars and religious souvenir shops. From behind the draped entrances waft the aromas of sweet-smelling spices and fragrant ground coffee.

60 A Greek Orthodox ceremony is conducted outside the Church of the Holy Sepulchre. The Greek Orthodox church controls the major part of the Holy Sepulchre, including the Tomb and Calvary. The Easter service at which the Patriarch receives God's 'Holy Fire' is a great attraction for the faithful. Pilgrims from all over the world gather to observe this ancient and mystical ceremony.

On the street corners are small stands selling the ubiquitous felafel, the local speciality which is a type of fried ground chick pea rissole, and pita bread stuffed with a variety of spiced vegetables and dressed with a little tahina or a deliciously hot spicy sauce. From David Street, turn into Chain Street which runs eastwards between the Jewish and Moslem Quarters, and you will come eventually to the impressive gates of Harem esh-Sharif, the Moslem name for 'the Noble Sanctuary', which covers approximately one-sixth of the total area of the Old Town. Within this huge walled enclave are some of Jerusalem's most important and historic buildings, which are of particular significance not only for Moslems but also for Christians and Jews, notably the Dome of the Rock, the Al-Aksa Mosque, and Solomon's Stables where the Crusaders once kept their horses and chariots. You cannot go to Jerusalem without visiting Harem esh-Sharif, not only because of its religious significance for Moslems as one of the holiest places of Islam but also for the exquisite beauty of the Dome of the Rock, which has come to symbolize the city of Jerusalem itself, like St Mark's in Venice or the Eiffel Tower in Paris. It is a spectacular building and one of the best surviving examples of seventh-century Islamic architecture. Built high on a hill above the city, it dominates Jerusalem with its beauty and splendour. No visitor seeing the Dome of the Rock for the first time can fail to be moved by its serene and richly decorated interior and the spectacular golden dome, which sparkles in the sunlight.

62 Near the Church of the Holy Sepulchre an Ethiopian priest solemnly carries a huge golden cross. Like the Syrians, the Ethiopians have access rights but no section of their own inside the gigantic church.

63 Inside the Church of St Mary Magdalene near the Garden of Gethsemane, a Russian Orthodox priest celebrates Mass. The church's distinctive golden onion domes make it one of the most easily recognisable in Jerusalem. Many of the faithful believe that the church stands on the site of the ascension – where Jesus rose up to Heaven.

64-65 *Two faces of religious belief in Jerusalem: the Russian Orthodox Patriarch (left) wearing a traditional icon on a chain; and an Orthodox Jew (right) praying beside the Wailing Wall, the most sacred and emotional symbolic monument in Judaism. Jews, Christians of all denominations, and Moslems all co-exist, albeit uneasily at times, in modern Jerusalem.*

66 From the Mount of Olives, you can get a spectacular view of the Old Town, its churches and mosques – even by moonlight as shown here.

67 This unusual concert is being staged in the Hassidic quarter of Jerusalem. Even in this Orthodox Jewish district, the young can relax and enjoy themselves by listening to popular music.

Although it is still sometimes wrongly referred to as the Mosque of Omar, the octagonal-shaped Dome of the Rock is not really a mosque at all. It was built in AD 691 by the Caliph Abd al-Malik who wanted to make Jerusalem the holiest city of Islam. The original dome was gilded with sheets of real gold, but now gilded aluminium sheets are used instead. Thirteen centuries later it is still one of the finest examples of early Islamic architecture. It was later decorated extensively inside by the sixteenth-century Ottoman Emperor Suleiman the Magnificent. The dome, mosaics, marble and stonework were completely restored in the 1950s and early-1960s through the initiatives of the Arab states in the region.

The Dome of the Rock was designed by Byzantine architects in the style of many typical Byzantine churches: in the form of two octagons, one within the other, radiating out from a circle topped by a gigantic dome. The outer cupola is now protected and decorated by sheets of bronze-aluminium whereas its interior is covered with mosaic tiles and some sixteenth-century stained glass. The upper exterior walls of the building are covered with glazed ceramic tiles in different shades of blue, indigo and turquoise with inscriptions from the Koran, while the lower walls are decorated with marble columns and pillars.

The sunlight filters into the sumptuous interior through the multi-coloured stained glass panels, predominantly of alternating gold, black and purple, which are in stark contrast to the holy rock itself which sits in the centre of the building surrounded by two concentric arched marble colonnades. On this golden block of stone, reputedly taken from the summit of Mount Moriah, Abraham prepared to sacrifice his son Isaac. It was also the place from which Mohammed ascended into heaven. Moslems believe that this caused the rock to break loose, only to be replaced by the Angel Gabriel whose fingerprints can still be seen on it, as can the hoof-prints of Mohammed's horse. Beside the rock stands a box containing hairs from the prophet's beard and underneath it is a cave, known as the Fountain of Souls, where many Moslems believe that the dead gather to pray. Thus the Dome of the Rock is an important religious symbol and a holy place for both Moslems and Jews.

Nearby on the Temple Mount is the most important mosque in Jerusalem – the silver-domed Al-Aksa Mosque which was built twenty years after the Dome of the Rock. If you want to visit this mosque, which has been destroyed by wars and earthquakes and rebuilt several times, you may not enter when prayers are being said. Although the cupola and some arches and prayer niches are decorated lavishly with mosaics and there are some elaborate stained glass windows, the interior is much simpler and less sumptuous than that of the Dome of the Rock. It was once a Royal palace for the Crusaders and the headquarters of the Templar Knights before reverting back to its original function as a mosque. Like the Dome of the Rock, it is a basilica desiged and built in traditional Byzantine style with the enormous decorated cupola suspended above several naves. When you enter the mosque, you must remove your shoes, and inside spread out on the floors are some of the most beautiful and precious hand-woven Oriental carpets in the world, creating a rich tapestry of bright colours.

68 The sun sinks in the evening sky behind the minaret of the Mosque of Al-Aksa. From this high tower, the muezzin summon the faithful to prayer five times a day. The largest mosque in the city, the silver dome is decorated inside with literally thousands of mosaic tiles.

69 The evening light falls on the spectacular Dome of the Rock, which is illuminated by moonlight.

70-71 Behind the narrow streets, labyrinthine alleys and age-old mosques and churches of the Old City, rise the new buildings and skyscrapers of the modern Jerusalem – the seat of Israel's government and centre of commerce.

72 Many Moslems unroll their prayer mats and pray in front of the Al-Aksa Mosque. Kneeling on the ground, they bow their heads towards the southern wall of the mosque in the direction of Mecca, the most holy shrine of Islam.

73 The Mosque of Al-Aksa, like other Byzantine-style basilicas, has several naves above which towers the decorated cupola. An interesting feature of the mosque is the plethora of brightly coloured oriental carpets; visitors must remove their shoes at the entrance.

74-75 Every Friday morning a great market is held close to Herod's Gate in the north of the Old City. Built by Suleiman the Magnificent, it was once thought (mistakenly as it turned out) that Herod's palace had stood on this spot.

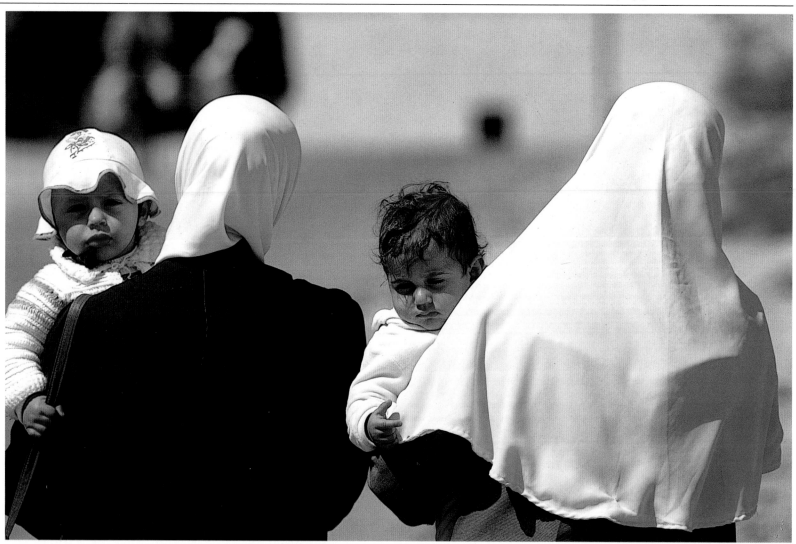

78 You can see Bedouin women of nomadic origin in traditional costume on the streets of Jerusalem, especially in the Moslem Quarter of the Old Town.

79 This Yemenite woman is wearing ceremonial dress. Yemenite Jews still account for a large community in Jerusalem. Although many had migrated to Palestine over the last few hundred years, the trickle of immigrants became a rush after the Israeli state was created. Their culture is deeply interwoven into the cultural fabric of Israeli society, and has particularly influenced Israeli folk music and dancing.

80 Women shop for food in the market of Mea She'arim in the heart of the Orthodox Jewish district. The ultra-Orthodox live in accordance with Jewish laws set down in the Torah. Their religious beliefs affect every part of their daily lives no matter how trivial. Orthodoxy, like religious fundamentalism elsewhere in the world, is growing in Israel, and many secular Jews are converting and adopting the ultra-Orthodox philosophy, dress and mores.

81 At the entrance to Mea She'arim, a sign exhorts women to dress modestly according to the dictates of the Torah. In observance with Jewish law, women must cover their heads with wigs or scarves and wear high collars, long sleeves and skirts below the knee. This applies to visitors to the quarter as well as residents.

83-83 In this Talmudic school, Torah Shomei Hachomot, the young scholars embark on the study and interpretation of the Holy Scriptures in accordance with the Torah's teachings.

84-85 *Even in the Jewish Quarter of the Old City where the ultra-Orthodox Hassidic Jews wear traditional dress (like the boy below and the strolling men right) there are new developments, albeit in a sympathetic style that will blend into their older surroundings.*

86 Top: At the Holyland West Hotel in West Jerusalem, there is a huge scale model of the ancient city as it was in AD 66, showing the Temple and other major buildings of the time on the eve of the Jewish uprising against the Romans.

86 Bottom: The ruined Citadel stands on the site of Herod the Great's palace which was erected in 24 BC. Archaeologists have uncovered the remains of the Phasael Tower, all that remained after the Palace was burned down in AD 66.

*I*t was on the slopes of the Temple Mount that Solomon built his temple circa 950 BC. However, it was later destroyed by the Babylonian king Nebuchadnezzar when he razed Jerusalem to the ground in 587 BC. A second temple was later built on the same site but this was desecrated and later demolished by Herod the Great. He subsequently built another temple there of which the Wailing Wall was an outer wall, with terraced courtyards and precincts. The Romans burnt the temple down in AD 70 and only the Wailing Wall – the holiest shrine in Judaism – remains. Here the pious come in their prayer shawls to pray or to write supplications on pieces of paper which they push into cracks in the wall between the large slabs of stone. These stones in the 50-foot high wall are smooth from the tears shed by Jews over many centuries, mourning the Temple's destruction.

From the Wailing Wall turn northwards through the Old City until you reach the Via Dolorosa, or the Way of the Cross, which is thought to be the route Jesus took when he carried his cross from the place of his trial to his crucifixion. It starts in the Moslem Quarter to the north of Harem esh-Sharif at the First Station of the Cross on the site of the Antonia Fortress which was once the administrative headquarters of the Romans. It was here that Jesus was tried and sentenced by Pontius Pilate. Today an Islamic boys' school stands on the site. There are fourteen Stations of the Cross in total with the final five Stations located in the Church of the Holy Sepulchre itself which was built on the site of Calvary. Although many historians doubt the authenticity of the sites, it is probable that Jesus followed a similar route, and pilgrims from all over the world retrace his footsteps along the Via Dolorosa, the

87 Top: The remains of the Citadel and Tower of David stand near the Jaffa Gate inside the Old City. Some of the buildings inside the Citadel now house the Museum of the History of Jerusalem complete with laser displays and scale models.

87 Bottom: The thick defensive walls of the eleventh-century Monastery of the Cross make it look more like a fortress than a church. The altar is reputed to stand on the site of a tree from which Christ's cross was made, hence the name.

Way of Sorrows, especially at Easter during Holy Week. Further along the road is the Second Station, the Monastery of the Flagellation, where Jesus was flogged by Roman soldiers and forced to wear a crown of thorns. It was here that he took up the cross and started out towards the place of his execution. The Third Station is where he first fell under its weight, and at the Fourth Station he encountered Mary in the crowd. Turn right at the next corner: the Fifth Station where the Romans commanded Simon of Cyrene to help carry the cross. At the Sixth Station further up the street, St Veronica wiped Christ's face with her veil. Continue on up the hill to the Seventh Station at the corner of Via Dolorosa and Souk Khan er-Zeit Street where Jesus fell for the second time. Outside the Greek Orthodox Chapel of St Chralampos is the Eighth Station where Jesus implored the women of Jerusalem not to weep for him. Proceed up a flight of stone steps to the Ninth Station where Jesus fell for the third time. The route then doubles back upon itself until you finally enter the Church of the Holy Sepulchre, erected on the hill of Calvary (Golgotha to the Greeks). Just inside the entrance, climb the steep steps and on the right is the Catholic Chapel: the Tenth Station where the Roman soldiers forced Jesus to strip and shared out his clothes among themselves. Here also, behind the altar, is the Eleventh Station where Jesus was nailed to the cross. The Twelfth Station is in the candlelit Greek Orthodox Chapel on the site where Jesus died on the cross. Outside the chapel, the Thirteenth Station marks the spot where he was taken down off the cross and Mary cradled his body in her arms. Below the centre of the large rotunda is a marble structure which covers the tomb in which Jesus was buried by

88 These modern 'nest homes' in the new quarter of Ramot near the Golan Heights are futuristic in style and make a startling contrast to the more familiar traditional architecture of Israel.

89 The Tomb of Theodor Herzl, the founding father of the Zionist movement, stands in a large park on the slopes of Mount Herzl together with the Herzl Museum. Every 14 May on Independence Day, a special ceremony is held here.

88

Joseph of Arimathea – the Fourteenth and final Station.
The Church of the Holy Sepulchre is unusual in so far as it is
shared by six religious denominations: the Roman Catholic, Greek
Orthodox, Armenian Orthodox and, less prominently, the Coptic,
Syrian and Ethiopian Churches. The original church was built on
this site in the fourth century by the Roman Emperor Constantine.
The church you see here now is the fourth one to be constructed
on this site and was built by the Crusaders in 1149. Far from being
a religious symbol for peace and unity, it has been fought and
squabbled over for centuries as the different Christian churches
vied with one another for control of this holy place. It can take up
to three hours to visit all the Stations, chapels, tombs and crypts.
Of particular significance are the Chapel of Adam, where Adam's
skull is reputed to be buried; and the Angel's Chapel where an
angel appeared to Mary Magdalene when she visited Christ's tomb
after the Crucifixion. On Easter Sunday, pilgrims gather in the
Church to witness a unique and extraordinary ceremony in which
the Holy Fire descends from Heaven. The Greek Orthodox
Patriarch emerges from the Holy Tomb with the fire from which
the faithful light their candles. For the believer, no visit to
Jerusalem is complete without visiting this holiest of places.
Jerusalem is a great and mystical city; the focal point of three of
the world's great religions. No other city can define its reason for
existence by faith alone, but this is the case with Jerusalem. For
thousands of years, it has moved countless people of different
faiths with its powerful beauty, its rich symbolism and its
timelessness, and it will continue to do so. Here, the past, present
and future meet and become indivisible.

90 Inside the Ohel Jiskor Hall – the Hall of Remembrance – at Yad Vashem, the memorial to the 6,000,000 Jews who died in the Nazi death camps, the stone-flagged floor is inscribed with the names of twenty-one extermination camps. In front of the Eternal Light is a vault containing the ashes of the martyrs of the camps.

91 Inside Yad Vashem is a permanent exhibition which bears testimony to the horror of the camps in photographs, newspaper cuttings, films and other archival documents of the period.

92-93 The distinctive white dome of the Shrine of the Book in the Israel Museum was designed by the American architects Frederick Kiesler and Armand Bartos. It was built to house the unique collection of Hebrew documents from circa 100 BC which are known as the Dead Sea Scrolls. Here also are the Book of Isaiah and letters written by the general who led the Jewish revolt against the Romans in AD132.

94-95 Jerusalem by night: the Old City walls and gates, churches and ancient buildings are lit up against the night sky.